Birds

Concept by Fran Bromage
Written and consulted by Camilla de la Bédoyère

Miles Kelly

Birds come in all shapes, sizes and colours. They live all over the world.

gull

seabird

boobook owls

southern crowned pigeon

crest

birds of prey

white-backed vulture
wing
beak
feathers
starlings
garden birds
Chico's tyrannulet
songbird
mute swan
flamingos
wading birds
waterfowl

stripy beak
puffin
ring-necked parakeet
scarlet macaw
tail feathers for display
common kingfisher
Feathers keep birds warm and help them fly. They can be very colourful.

crown
blue jay
plumage
long tail
purple heron
courting display
red wattle
peacock
pheasant
train

stooping
peregrine falcon
buzzard
soaring
great blue heron
flapping
hovering
mountain hummingbird

American
kestrel
swallow
agile
night hunter
barn owl
bird of prey
hyacinth
macaw
Most birds can fly.
They flap their
strong wings to get
into the air.

woodland bird
rainforest bird
tawny
owl
Philippine eagle
flightless
bird
kakapo
varied
thrush
ground-dwelling
migratory
bird

toco toucan
tropical bird
harpy eagle
perching
Forest and woodlands are perfect places to see and hear birds.
blue-and-gold macaw
wood pigeons
pecking

strawberries
western tanager
insect
blackbird
flycatcher
goldfinch
nuts
teasel
seeds
bird feeder

woodpecker
osprey
sharp talons
acorns
Some birds eat seeds, flowers and bugs. Other birds hunt bigger animals to eat.
fish
nectar
hummingbird

All birds lay eggs. Most birds make a nest, where they keep their eggs until they hatch.
weaverbird
woven nest
grass
house sparrows
flock
entrance
duck
ducklings

bald eagles
messy nest
twigs
burrowing owl
burrow
collared dove
clutch of eggs

Farmyard birds **peck** at their food on the ground. They lay eggs and look after their chicks.

cockerel
comb
dangling wattle
turkey
pecking
chicken
corn
chicken coop
scratching

snowy owl
Arctic
emperor penguins
Antarctic
golden eagle
mountains
The place where a bird lives is called its habitat. Birds live in many habitats.
ostrich
savanna
scarlet ibis
jacana
wetland